Any Keep or Contour

Any Keep or Contour

Audrey Bohanan

WAYWISER

First published in 2019 by

THE WAYWISER PRESS

Christmas Cottage, Church Enstone, Chipping Norton, Oxfordshire, OX7 4NN, UK
P.O. Box 6205, Baltimore, MD 21206, USA
https://waywiser-press.com

Editor-in-Chief
Philip Hoy

Senior American Editor
Joseph Harrison

Associate Editors
Eric McHenry | Dora Malech | V. Penelope Pelizzon | Clive Watkins
Greg Williamson | Matthew Yorke

Copyright © Audrey Bohanan, 2019

The right of Audrey Bohanan to be identified as the author of this work
has been asserted by her in accordance with the
Copyright, Designs and Patents Act of 1988.

All rights reserved. No part of this publication may be reproduced, stored in
a retrieval system, or transmitted in any form or by any means, electronic,
mechanical, photocopying, recording, or otherwise, without the prior permission
of both the copyright owner and the above publisher of this book.

9 7 5 3 1 2 4 6 8

A CIP catalogue record for this book is available from the British Library

ISBN 978-1-904130-95-6

Printed and bound by
T. J. International Ltd., Padstow, Cornwall, PL28 8RW

again, for Jeff

Acknowledgments

Grateful acknowledgment is made to the editors of the journals in which these poems or slightly different versions of them have appeared:

Birmingham Poetry Review: "Counter-Boys," "Horse Farm in Winter," "Streamer Handle-Grips in the Wind"

Colorado Review: "Ever-Missing"

E.D. #78, Found Undelivered: "Autumn's Modular Elliptic Curves"

The Iowa Source: "Children in Hurricane Weather"

The Hopkins Review: "Mother of Richard"

Passager: "Winter School"

Sewanee Theological Review: "Home Colony"

*

"Girl, Imperfectly Perennial" appears as character witness testimony in the Madera Superior Court Record, case #CR07823, People vs. Jacob Lee Travis.

*

The author wishes to give thanks to Emilia Dahlin in acting on behalf of the Marion Weber Beyond Boundaries Flow Fund for an endowment that provided assistance during the writing of this book.

With gratitude in great measure to Mark Edelstein, Joe Harrison, Phil Hoy, and Laurel MacDuffe for essential encouragement along the way.

Contents

I.

Gorge of Eels	13
The Far Beyond with Indigo Buntings	14
In a Moonless Darkness	16
Drowning-Traps by Time Lapse	17
Home Colony	18
Winter School	20
Ever-Missing	21
Ridiculous Spring	23
The Small Sparrows of the Spandrels	24
Counter-Boys	25
Girl, Imperfectly Perennial	26
Horse Farm in Winter	28
Balanced Like a Shadow-Line	29
In the Time of Shortbread	30

II.

The Quarry of You	33
Fifteen as Seen Before	34
Streamer Handle-Grips in the Wind	35
Of Unmodified Pink-Hided Mules	36
While Those on the Docks Drove Pilings	37
Cat Jupiter	38
In a Mountain Pass	39
Where Antlers Are Left	40
A Surgical Inconsistency	41
To Kill a Cowbird	43
Contour and Keeping	45
Late Tension	47
Of Winter School, of Irene	48
At Sixes and Sevens	50

III.

To Be Shaken Out of a Life	53
All the Small Clavicles	54
Of Within, Bleak of Winter	56
Owls' Eggs	57
Canyonland Under Clerical Scrutiny	58
Mother of Richard	60
Just Above the Water	61
William in Undermeal Atmosphere	62
Soft-Footed Fictions	64
Of Schoolroom Ceremony	65
Mourning Dove by Herself	66
Children in Hurricane Weather	67
Autumn's Modular Elliptic Curves	68
Hayfields, Height-of-Land	69

NOTES	73

A NOTE ABOUT THE AUTHOR	75

I.

Gorge of Eels

There, in the far upstream, in the wilderness
of the autonomous, a mirroring gulf
of who I most likely was had been lapping

alone along its hollowed shore in the likes
of a fish story – as slacktide as when I
went out for River-wolf Pike, that was what I

had said. As though I could take my word for it.
I was grasping for chocks in my outermost
Newfoundland gorge of plotline by leap of faith

down a chasm-drop as the sun was setting.
In a lull, this was how I had thought of it.
While all the while it grew late, and fictive of

my intention, deep in the precarious.
What I had said, like the eel you hook, what you
reel up instead out of a mist, there was no

annulling of it. And like an eel, it pulled
out of my grip in a heap of slavering.
After some long while I had to cut it free.

In a duskdown on empty-handedness was
where I had been, in my small isolation.
Which then fell away. Like the white wakefulness

welts of scar tissue fall into, the metal-
bound grief you must carry in the cheek of you, it
did not stop falling once I could speak again.

The Far Beyond with Indigo Buntings

"And so when we examine a nest,
we place ourselves at the origin
of confidence in the world."

– Gaston Bachelard

There is no sparing of the always thinking
out. Time, now, for the emptiness of their nest
to be filled with the sound of small wings under
big thunder. There is no picking the past tense

out, as fused as oil of myrrh put anywhere
close to Nei silk, the bond becomes eternal
as the future. It is solid. They are gone,
by feel by now they are flying, by tonight

they will be heading out across the spillage
of constellations in the South sky, which they
keenly skirt beyond the concrete of, as slick
as a sublingual curative in dodging

the complexities of the spleen. All in how
they bushwhack around the more damply hummocked
brain regions. She wove in Sweet Canary Grass
to ride the sundown tipped in crimson waves, scent

of Lady's Drawer from fields mown inland, upland
by the tide, to gather them back to high ground.
And to meet the mid-rib, there she laid in fur,
kill of Cottontail or jumping-mouse to be

sorrowed after. To keep the hearts of the young
from being broken, so they will be broken
less often. I am not fitting their dark flight
to my makeshift bind of comprehension as

The Far Beyond with Indigo Buntings

little backdoor collection agency claims
on the soul. Nothing there can be returned to.
While in their coverts they keep safe each likeness
the stars come up with deeper than scar tissue.

In a Moonless Darkness

I had gone south for awhile and into the dark
of cotton-mouthed caves beyond the reach

of ultraviolet's daylight Braille. I was looking
to be drawn by a deep displacement to those

who from the start have been confined
to a sightless interior, to those without overlap

of speech. To see how those whose hands must be
both eyes and voice retrace their way up out of

an underground as would a mine-canary left behind to flail
what remains of its wingspan. To see from a blankness

of canvas with no carrier-oil to pool in clots of pigment.
I was rethinking the dark, north of daylight on the hillside

where the herd slept, where I'd gone to wake them
from a vapored sleep. Of the earliest hours

and the hill spine splaying open to the story in which
the wolf does not turn tail, the dog is not down-home bound

in the end. Where there were chimney ruins of cellar holes
and rock maples dragged by their limbs

up into the night sky like those who say goodbye
with both hands waving. Waving back to the small

conditional, with plans that could still be made,
while all along elsewhere daylight had been spoken for

from the start, not once to come lunging to its feet.

Drowning-Traps by Time Lapse

There was a while when I had come across
a trespass, in that time unfamiliar
enough to be vile, first by whereabouts
and half again by kind. There, in deep woods,
in a hemlock brook, drowning-traps for mink

had been line-strung, and not by anyone
who shared my eye-for or need for blood cure,
root-crossed as refuge and thrush-prone, of flutes
and vowelled notes they hold over snag-holes,
as witch-wands are held, so the sapwood strips.

Diapente, an electuary
for an ill-will cure, it was a place for
outdistancing. Moreso, of the winch truck
bottomed-out in its deep primevalness
of club moss in a hush – by its ear-split

it could bend a thrush's breathless egg in
half. In that time I knew a wasting rage
and sleepless nights, as witness to Enhanced
Techniques of Interrogation as seen
to, by drop-light. I was as was the mink,

unclawed and sunken like a channel stone.
There I fell beneath that spell awhile while
I took things *as personal to myself*.
But all of that lies in the long-ago
when I believed so in an eye-to-eye.

Home Colony

> *In the space and time that he broods over in one flight, a single summering is heresy. It is likewise the scandal of painter and poet, who bring seasons together at that height where all intersect.*
>
> St.-John Perse, "The Bird,"
> translated by Robert Fitzgerald

There is no real malice nor any mincing
of it to speak of when rupture and render

take to the sky between the trigger-finger
and one's own flock flying safely home. Only

much to say from beyond the gerrymandered
bounds of childhood and its failed state, and little

said of it. Where the past rewinds its harm, now
in the closer focus of it, I cannot

say this to the nonetheless dead and wounded.
To keep a colony, swallow family,

swept to its house when subject to predation,
to be vigilant in it calls for gunfire.

If the nights since have been threaded through the reach
of crosshairs, if I no longer sit with those

shot, of the starling family, where they lay
in tall grass to die, reconciliation

must rise there, by nature a speaking in tongues,
none of which needs be slit for the vocables

of forgiveness to be swept up and air-borne.
By blotted script, by cursive murmuration

of wings sweeping them skyward in the late hour,
unwronged by writ, by stay of execution.

Winter School

In rutted November when leaf mold softened
off the shoulders of bad roads, when field mice pried
their way inside sideways and the deer grew thin,
sometime around then when the school bus we rode
would stop going down into the bottomland
for the season, not that it wasn't a fen,
and not that we hadn't been once by then, or
maybe twice, as far in as the only ground
to turn around on and pulled into the ditch
and out again while most of us probably
ranked on the rest from the Bog Road who so much
as told us they knew no better than hot dogs,
root beer Kool-Aid in screw-jars for breakfast, or
took it from those who lived worse, being field-poor
and ledge-ridden, brought up in dirt-floor kitchens,

when the wheels spun in the soft edge, every one
of us would be watching out the back in case
some last kid not quit of it might come running
up out of that slough as if it weren't a lot
drawn so early on, like drawing the ribs up
through a bone-dog put too young on a snub-chain,
it had shaped him, as if he could flee how he
got there the same as they all fled a house fire
one lost at least most of his ear from, before
we'd turn back to the hard-packed with none of those
who lived there, and later when we'd lie awake
beneath the eaves, for all we hadn't spoken
so it soured like mist stuck in a rookery,
we weren't about to miss the lot of them, not
if we had to think of them down-in all winter.

Ever-Missing

To speak of them is a delicate, eggshell
affair, can appropriate nearness in a creeping
larceny of close-footing unless you are

an intimate acquaintance. Often the mist
must come to lie thick and tangled, covetous
over a striplot, before care of a spoken kind

can be offered to transfuse, to put up
its whispered, viscous resistance. By when,
its sole authority has long since set out alone

and barefoot in a lambprint nightgown,
against odds of loss and legtrap, of where,
in which few miles the one house will appear,

and of how well-lit the abrupt stairwell.
Here let it be a hurried truth, that
proximity need not peel the self away

wholesale just because the heart does.
Where the schoolyard Halloween party paraded
downhill, the doorfronts were paler, fatigued

toward the yellow-once of marrow. One of many
such Chicken Towns with its child of factory
process, blue damage-dye effluent, whose

costume armscyes have been handsewn
in a silk-twist. Later is the hour that comes
least specifically, like a ground-fog

among the trees left, like a half-reason,
blister-rust. Some, not always just those
around their evening fire, hold ever

Ever-Missing

to the utterance, Where home had best
have been paying more attention, it is
a pity-trough to meddle in, and morbid.

I have become wary where the brain-pan
fills to its shallow edge, narrowly thematic,
a spillway. Expedience is quick to say,

put her absence to rest in a nest of epic
proportions. In a lofty clutch of turn-
taking, as with owls' eggs so plumb

to the same axis that one of the awakened
young can become, can devour another. It
is that likely place from which to say

I hardly knew her. Your bunting-child
now, your wind-blown broom-straw, once
born, once swept away and stolen.

Ridiculous Spring

Now all through the night you will be walking off
your heavy-heartedness, dark as your soul-mare
in a black internalized bleed, up and down

the barn floor. Time, some would say, to relinquish
hope as the failed trial-cultivar mixed in with
self-sown, maladaptive anger grown wild on

its own. They would be telling you, walk her up
and down the end-grain until there is no blame
left to lay out, or else it's running it all

over again as lappet-moths beat their wings
to tissue-scar up against the windowpanes
and coyotes waste their eye-wicks, closing in

around the field's edge. Come time, and they will be
telling you, give up on the run of bad-luck
clover, twisted-gut regret or we won't be

telling you again. I am not the one to
speak differently, only tonight could be
a hallowing of owls, the moon is still young

enough to save face. As tomorrow is put
at risk by vials of treachery-in-waiting
in the wings for daybreak crowed and clattering

her hooves down to the barn floor, before that, in
the having of words, of the ridiculous,
this is not it, this is not going to be it.

The Small Sparrows of the Spandrels

When it came down to blood-red as bled only
in the abstract among the neatstock and flocks,
from what I'd been told and up to my boot tops

by halflight, then it was time that I went cold
on killing. There is no blood seepage that pools
so shallowly as to be undershot, caught

and carried up on the vanes of a concept
as on the flat of a color-wheel surface.
It was in a venous darkness that I found

my way by feel, as though I had come to pass
through an open-work of chicken-wire without
that which was not in me. The First Methodist

Edition of architectural constraints
had pictured arches grown over in blackthorn.
It was said of their possible side-effects

that the spandrels of them infilled with angels
in following after. Here I was also
home-churched to ignore the flutter of despair,

in the cornering of small sparrows, to catch,
to hold them by their legs and to dispatch them
broadsidedly against the grey of fenceline.

Yet this I could not do. Mine was to go on
under a sky-full, so poor was my grasp of
that which is only there only more air-borne.

Counter-Boys

Both are blue-eyed, backwater boys and steady
of keel as in a harbored chop running close

to the surface. Through the screen door, we have been
watching the light glare, going acetylene

on domestic crime, cruiser broadside out front,
as they say in a hush, are quick to tell me

it is his own son, luck of the draw, the cop
is putting in handcuffs, ducking his head down.

These are the boys who choose to be soft of speech
and clear in their position. They are making

sure I have no doubt that their sympathies lie
with the father, that they plan to disembark

on solid ground, light out for territory
with no categories of predation. They

say, because they sweep after breakage, the son
is the piece of glass that sticks in the father's

throat, and they can see, as some say you can see
when a nuclear explosion leaves a sketch

of the deeper, skeletal structure of those
around you, which hand they themselves will land in,

that it never was not this way, they will leave
the whole shattering, boundless sea behind them.

Girl, Imperfectly Perennial

Both here and gone she was for a given time,
cupped inside the hollow of a mussel shell

to be spooned out like a dry volumetric
of known quantity, last seen in gold sandals.

Possibly, for awhile, a body can be
pinned down in location, as when the petals

of a schoolgirl wish mark the underfootage
where they have fallen. Now, deep into winter,

the garden below the snow is webbed in veins,
a courthouse artist's rendition in a sketch

of its satin-beaded budded full-bloom form
put down in a tin-type, graven as is my

retinal burn of her as she was last left
aflame in a fig-orchard. To have been held

for a brief season, to have been palpable
as the lipids in a thin film of ash spread

beneath the foliage could only keep her
here in a final form of hostage-taking.

Where is it written, that snow will bring release
of wrist and ankle into the mist of earliest

hours, of the first pastels down the border length;
that she will become the crush of monarda

into irises blue recesses, of columbine
running its spurs through all the tones to either

Girl, Imperfectly Perennial

side of rose-red, that red will be no less red
than is the winter of her still unworldly;

that, of carex, rheum, asarum, I will
come to know them like the back of her girl-hand.

Horse Farm in Winter

A chill advances like a borrowing against the harvest
in cropland when engines altogether shut down,
winter-killed in a lower pasture, a horse farm story.

A stake-bed, backhoe, and plow truck go quiet.
Which tells of a hole filled, which means
no remarks have been made in closing.

Where cinquefoil and saw-grass have been
hayed off the margins in a forethought of winter mulch
for burial, first-crop is up around the barn

where the herd is, with hardly a way around the one –
and this one is shanky and lean, a buckskin apart
from the rest of them – who is halfway down the field

in a blinding stare. You cannot get around the one
who loves overly. One left to stand alone as the snow
starts falling. How long, how soon lost in the grey of it.

Balanced Like a Shadow-Line

I cannot speak of where to, what pool
an undercut of loss spills into once it is done
with the well of the lower eyelid. Here,
they have come home to a flatland floodplain,

her mother wing-tipped and torn as a Mourning-Cloak
and she, the wild-horses-could-not daughter,
most recently parked for life in the keeps
of a pinstriped wheelchair, of paralysis.

Here, under the canopy of sugar maples,
in a green gulf of shade, there is no kicking
of the cross she is bearing, there is
no sickle-carrying anywhere here,

dressed blackly in its full-length of blame.
That they will sit here where the floodplain
is a blood-chamber of on-going fill and emptying.
That out of the blue come zinc-whites

in the foreground of the garden, a saturation
of crimsons, green before bronze of the cornfields
in a middle-ground of shadow-line,
without which there would be the river

and the hills beyond and likely less anticipation
of them. And when she says she doesn't know,
she may never know why this happened, she speaks
as though, when the river has a bend to take

it's no different from the ribbon-curl memory makes;
she speaks as though somewhere in the long ago
she has grasped the full length
of her own deep structure beforehand.

In the Time of Shortbread

I have heard it said before, for some there is
no escaping the while when one finds oneself
lost in a forest of primeval anger,
fungal as is one's own undoing. I woke

to such as this as one whose fate had been told
unsolicited: it was said that all my
coordinates would be lost and enlarged off
the map's edge where, also, the scale was. Also

was said, this would come like a white squall of fault
to hollow out a skeletal silhouette
where the self was. As a footnote was mentioned
my incidental survival of it. First

I would fall full under the spell of telling.
Years were then to go by as good as largely
gone. It was a haunting I could not skim off
by the close-at-hand, but like the memory

of icing brought to a boil and consistent
with the dead give-away as pearled on shortbread,
it could break to the touch, such that some are moved
to eavesdropping extremes. This came as if I

had caught my eye in a cottage window nick
of shutter-speed, when I dared look into it.
Then rage was on the run, witch-hunted deeply
into the iris. Then *lost* had just begun.

II.

The Quarry of You

Only by lifetimes later as I went back
to the same abyss of mass and tremor-stone,
of disruption wrenched out of shattering core,

only then could I see how my singular
dimension of you once saw a falconed place
for predator and prey to meet out over

the whole of what you would ever need to know
or ask of me to be good for. In that time
it had grown all too late to claim those poorest

of dispensations. The snow was now melting
off. By the wild light caught in each falling drop
as a surge of happiness is caught, briefly,

no longer could I for long lose sight of what
love is there for. For all the outcropped tailings
carted off, for the softening of fir-moss

where the shade deepened, for the sky's bull's-eye blue,
what of any thought of love had you not thought
to write, what thought would I have written back to.

Fifteen as Seen Before

There is no fixing here of age-related,
of duffle-bagged for Sunday evening exchange
at the gas pumps on the edge of town. A girl

is sacked, made awkward on long legs by luggage,
by inelegant off-put of custody.
There is an arc to it when silence winds up

like a hay-truck fuel pump still found here, out back
in the flatland, in-between trips, meant only
to fill a reserve. At the heart of refuge

sought out privately, where the kerf of a field
being mown circles closer to the center
each time, can harm be done to a hidden fawn.

Her mother now makes baggage-room, and meanwhile
is her father gone to make a purchase. She
is left to move on, in smaller engagements

of traction toward home where, in fiction, someone
likely would be there to tell her, all told, all
of her will be left of her come tomorrow.

Streamer Handle-Grips in the Wind

Like open-weave wicker-work an infant is
left in, out in a fine mist on a doorstep,
regret is structured for over-exposure
in more than the short run. Now it is later

on, while a wind whips uphill, gale-force around
the corner of the barn. It makes for itself
a wildness of visible identity
given to fury in streamer handle-grips

on a bicycle parked cherry-red out front.
By now he would be beyond transport by them.
Time was when he would ride like the wind downhill
into the hollows, to return to a place

he was once known to. Only now, later-on,
no one lives there any longer. Once fury
is unlit and parked to the back of the barn,
once you have been the wind, you do not speak of it.

Of Unmodified Pink-Hided Mules

If contempt should burn its marrow-acid through
to the quick, if scorn should, let it remain true
that, in theory, all conspiracy narrows
down to the known. They know this, they who redo
the deep interior of things by gilding

with a gold paint-chip choice of genetic code.
Its taking place goes on while neighbors upstream
repair a garage door opener, out late
in the yard with floodlights on a lumbering
down of ricks. In this backland, it is spoken

of broccoli's chalk-outline, its billowed singe
of crop-dusting flown through it from the inside.
And all the while meanwhile, blood-pumpkins run wild
to breed back from the catalog four-in-hand.
In the field-guide to green and the drift of it,

as long as the code is binary, draft-mules
will graze in these spinney-woods of betony
and witch-broom, ham-shouldered asses bred ahead
through great white Percherons, and their hides and eyes
will be pink. They will be no less hushed, less held

than summer-colts off a lunge-line, and like haze,
they will not be brought back to where they came from.
Like a dream you wake from, a candle-lit cake
down a woodland stream once you wade in your rose-
ringed dress to have it, they too will then be gone.

While Those on the Docks Drove Pilings

The swill of it, to have a country cave in.
There is among us a frayed strand and gutted
of neurological material, where
faulty wiring arcs across a drop. Maroon
fumes where the ends have been seared. When the rope-boys
behind the counter in the rock-climbing store
would singe the ravels of neoprene, breathing
in all day long, life expectancy was sheared
off, and morbidly. In the hog belt, by metes
and bounds, all is off compass, all is in hogs.
For this I would not miss a day in the rocks
above with the slatey juncos piping up
their courage like the clan of Ross going on
nothing but wild sound, marching down in full dress.

Cat Jupiter

After near certain ruin, after foul moments
in which the soul has grown as undemonstrative
as grey effusion in an inconclusive x-ray,
when paralysis of the self has set in,
there is little speaking then of flight-plan
alternatives, like those of buntings
who only in dreams will veer
from the constellations. Here,
fate takes on the sensory, a wreath

of sparrow-spray over a stone pool,
as with any change of state
to be seen through. In the beyond,
across the mown field, there once had been
a plank-bridge, inviolable when it
came to tonnage, and where once
a load of logs in passing beneath its truss-work
was caught in a running-chain twist,
in a snap of logs

put air-borne and slowed
into a space of open sky out over water.
In the soundless, in their long roll
of falling away was a cat streaking out
ahead of them and clear, to home,
to her door, to put her face safely
to a knot-hole on the kitchen floor.
A holding of herself close to fate,
her burnishing the weathered signage of it.

In a Mountain Pass

Soured roadside in a mountain pass diner
is the wilderness by cubic inch, by brood
of trophy-fawns under glass. You well may quell

fits of cut-throat narrative with a fine blind-stitch,
but never will you spot-clean poor in taste, crude
as an oil spill is quietly violent.

Always there is plot one table over, of
written elsewhere, as a father lifts his hand,
but only slightly, and the son no longer

objects to pre-emption by food groups not
of his choosing. In county courthouse hallways,
in places of folding chairs set aside for

character-driven storyline, here motive
pales when put to public display. While elsewhere,
in deep woods, a vireo goes by passion

that is private, and sings himself out of breath.
That far from the realm of hummingbirds pressed flat
toward the back of a book, it is that quiet.

Where Antlers Are Left

There, was where he now was, by lay of the bones
of him spread out in a long-bed along with
oil of bar and chain, to end up with pump-jacks

his spine curved around in a softening
of the blow that death must bring. The spine, and
then the deer-shed, as it is put, in the active.

We were leaning over him as when there are
three to bear witness it is nearly foregone,
of a connection to the everlasting,

to shepherd-legends having three who set out
empty across the desert sands, and one stride
says they will find him alive while another

puts further off the fireside, earlier
is the sundown, of sky to be lacquered shut.
It is not written how hearts stuck in their throats

at daybreak. Yet they knew. There are the minor
landslides of anticipation, an infill
beforehand, as when footprints in front of them

caved in from behind the heel. So that by when
they arrived at what was left of him, they knew.
A whitetail dies in dormancy, in the lean

of late fall, by starvation. Softly he lay
down, nose to tail, a stream-stretch where the last late
red dragonflies would have lighted in one-by's,

where an ox-bow took on a ripple-effect
with the sun still on it, into the shadows.
This by positive identification.

A Surgical Inconsistency

Come time, not this time, forgiveness is likely
to arrive in a line-storm. I am not through

with him, he who was mordant harm done to her
in the name of cure, inflictive, more dorsal

than a fin-in-waiting, incalculable
to her as winds off-shore. In the privacy

of his practice, he broke her down in pieces,
openly, a field-cot treatment to the back

of the tent. They never said judgment could not
be quick to file its own grievances under

someone else's skin, and I have not slackened
in the wallowing view of him as fitting

his practice through a phone line, putting distance
to the narrows of his predicates in one

after another, each to be followed-up
by scalpel in a random of glandular

revisions, over and over. What was left
of her was largely gone. Only, her courage

stayed as long with her as indigo further
out than would-be stars are. She was a Monarch,

wind-torn of wing, taking on the blue ocean,
all of which was out to sea. There she sat and

let the phone ring at her until illness was
as imaginary as a phantom sense

A Surgical Inconsistency

of mountain to be flown through. I have no way
of carving out a soft spot in destiny

to stand in for her as a soul-donor, nor
can I snake his coil of claims back through their wire

of blackened passageway. Nor, come tomorrow,
will I be kinder, will his intent float free

as raft-kelp; will I say it differently:
let him, as well, catch what he can be good for.

To Kill a Cowbird

Fault and the finding of it are a brood,
more parasitic than a nested egg

hatched out of place. It begins like a lark
singing over fallow ground, but never

does it look good. In the interior
of side-taking, in the shell-game of it,

some few would pick the satin-shouldered birds
along the pond's edge, and side with harm done

to the smaller Yellowthroats who have been
compromised by rigs of competition.

I once had thought to tie a falconry
of principle to Virtue's wrist. I wore

its church-glove, and blindly pledged dominion
of the nickel-buffalo and plains-wars.

No less was my sense of goodness than of
trains and tunnel-speed in sixth-grade math, or

of its chill and condensation. Yet of
soft decay from the buck-and-wing of eyes

pecked out as if in hatred, so grievous
do some find this that my sister, for one,

would first live-trap the less favored of them –
in her cultural twist of the oar-locks,

always was she one for turning into
the current in a river-crossing, quick,

for instance, to club to death woodchucks by
age five, not more than six – and secondly,

she'd drown them after in her kitchen sink,
even though she is the smart one, and so

must know as well as I do what mired
weave of moss and larch it is if first you

let the huge, feathered angel of the heart
fold-to its towering wings and settle

next to you over-closely. The rueing
then, the rivet-tin put to a hot flame

to keep the seat beside the heart empty,
what seep of shadowed pond you then fly to.

Contour and Keeping

Four, so she decides. Wisp of a decision,
grasp of the thin green gust she goes riding down
silk-driven, and carried alive in her. To

the kitchen window. One of the comb-footed
kind, spider with her own witch-wand to follow,
little sphere of gyres to place her on the glass.

I'll never know how so. And here she takes up
her spinning. Taking care of involves at least
some small pillaging, cold as a humid draft

through the ribs. Not again I won't be sitting
strung along clots of slogged and dawn-cracked, of boot-
legged themes, those that speak of short-handed fair

when it comes to fairer treatment: for months she
tends all four of them, thinnest membrane of touch
keeping contact, a kind of singing to them,

smoky shape-notes she sings back to the wood thrush.
His lung-full for them to sleep within, without
her. For this she has been built to excess in

her count of many legs, all the better to
comb out day and night that which is not spider.
Combing against the hollow interior,

their keep of vellum-thin. As it is written,
privilege of valid design principles,
fragile and loaned out guardedly like a first

edition handbook on what is kept inside
the nature of contour and proportion, food
on the table, stone-fruits, bread – she does not stop

Contour and Keeping

in her constant handling of them. So the leaves
begin to fall. Her hatchlings, little footnotes,
so they come and go. In the end, one vellum

is left blank and hanging on the sash. Is left:
her slow starvation by click-beetle stash gone
falling out of reach. Long silences of my

hesitation, how by blood, up to our crooks
of elbows in silted pockets of it we
are distantly related. I have been sprung

close at hand from that leg-poor species as is
cultural, as is cradled from the thicker
porcelain of a Petri dish, hardened off,

hung out on a pallet-board in a cold front
porch room. By culture schooled to ride and shoot, to
hang wallpaper. A hatchling of the kind born

into the keeping of a few, fewer good
appendages, I am her undersigned, her
leafless to be left behind beyond the glass.

Late Tension

Here, in an early cell-division stage
of human endeavoring, in a Coin Mat laundry,
a small boy stands unauthorized in a folding chair,
eager to help fold clothes. In the splintering-off
of his making, in the marrow of him,
he well may grasp that all is preparation,
that some tomorrow will come the schoolyard bully
to get the drop on him, that any future
is a twisted strand of doubt, any barbaric enough
might skin him away in the stirrup-tangle
of a lock-step holding pattern if his horse
is rangy and throws him through it.
That it is in him, in the incremental
lesson plan, for the ever-present
he has leaned forward, and in a moment
comes the critical reprimand, with which he
now hides his face in his forearms
to sink himself slowly into a shame of tears
he must contain. All the salt runs off
while he is up to his elbows and easily lost
inside the smallness of himself. And some
may be quieted with the stale of anodyne
and cheese from the choices vended, and some
can only hide in the darkness of their vulnerability
like the daytime stars in the depths
of childhood's well, of all the given marvels
they know themselves to be full of.

Of Winter School, of Irene

She was of groundswell, the green
of wetland seeps in early spring,
                and catastrophically mistaken

for one who is forgone. Sorrow
of those spoon-fed truths and their tarnishings
                had said instead she was by then as lost

as the dark-eyed mink in such approximations
of necessity as drowning-traps: she'd know
                no difference, needn't worry. You worry

what anyone will be found by. In times
such as that one, candor often come cleanest
                first-handed. From the older girls

we knew Irene of the lowground had been led
away, terror-stricken as the splint-shinned mare
                you blindfold uphill from winter's pit;

that in a cell-block cellar, in its gray-lit home
of economics, of brine in its tinned tub
                of salts and shame, they were made

to take her bone-chip button clothing
off her in a lesson-plan of uncleanliness,
                that this not be but assumed

of her, or found inaccurate. That the skin
should be scrubbed out of fissures,
                as these do scavenge along the tracks

for poor of quality. She had been put
into the tub. Dismantled, salt-rub
                in the wound of humiliation,

as the older girls would tell you.
Did not come back to school again,
>   that she knew enough not to return to.

At Sixes and Sevens

All through the woods the paper birches now bend
doubly as do arcs of plotline weakened by
overextension: I have had the story
of he who was all my father all wrong by
way of an ending – as if it could be told
parabolically, as when the pencil

is hung on a string. And now winter so soon
has turned southward in half-profile. Here is March,
the time of straw-matted oxen, heavier
about the eyelids, nosing the stone they pull,
and a fourth away from spring and grief lodged fast
in the passageway through the kitchen. I had
put in asides, how the kitchen had once been

a pigsty, the spoon he had put down beside
the single teacup left that day, by the sink.
Of the sheets left line-blown, the floral pattern
snapping. That he fell his full length through childhood,
there in the house he was born in, when I meant
was last on his shoulder, high in summer pasture.

III.

To Be Shaken Out of a Life

"To be among the shaken
is to have responded
to grimly disturbing experiences..."

– Andrew Shanks

Longing, and close on its heels despair
hits a trip-wire where hope has been driven off

like a hare on the run and strung low
to the ground under a shadow's wingtips.

When there is not anywhere left to arrive at,
hope separates like porridge-peas

gone too cold to ever reach the table,
never the infant not yet nine days old

clutched on a shoulder in the freezer aisle
corrugations of a box store, dilute wines

and one of the known food groups accounted for
in the cart he is carried over, with no

crocheted intervention, no metabolic spelling
of his skin, and he is shivering. To be

a crib-death survivor, an infant
would have to be shaken out of his life

and back into one that is different;
shaken out into a darkness like a single cell

when catastrophe is sea-deep. Then he must go
by hand over hand back into the pod of him.

All the Small Clavicles

Now, in the Anthropocene, may there not yet
come a wreck in train of thought, or soon may it
quit the habit of making a wish make do
for a fathom-cure where everywhere oceans
sit chalked for salvage. In the deep, all thinking

is cellular and of a single mind. There,
for the diatomaceous among us, law
sets no limit on size, as in the long-since
when those bonneted and brim-capped were sent out
cold by sootlight for millwork, down the backstair.

Long has atmosphere been what they are up to,
deep in the photic zone of brine and brackish.
Change comes there in black as once in red it did
on the quilling-room floor. It moves in silence
quick as milfoil by boatkeel from pond to pond.

Day by day it grows dark by way of shoulders
stood upon, of those who once lived among us
in the next town over. By architecture
of human collision will a bindweed hedge
wind there, and never can it quickly enough

take down the brickwork of a town, of the mills
of it taken afterward, after plywood.
Where those of the smallest shoulders shouldered-up
like porcelain on a cup-shelf, the push-broom
of wreckage sweeps knee-deep out to sea, a slew

of lawn chairs legs and piecemeal for an ocean.
And I mean to get away with some Seven
Faults-Cognitive when I say that, because I,
too, was once of that soft-shelled age, on a lark
and launched into moonlight by creel-boat, this was

All the Small Clavicles

toil also, and for waxed-papered fish and bread
with the engine cut at high noon, why we threw
the short-catch back was the sea was nobody's
ocean. That I may have been well-lunchboxed off,
but I can tell you, even a child could get it.

Of Within, Bleak of Winter

To hold to what one knows, blur and whitescape
of snowfall in the clearing, bare of motive,

clean of sweep. Coyotes somewhere thick in the pines
deep out of sight slathering down on a doe, a mother-of

past her prime. From this one would do well to bleed off
a shallow of red imperative, no more than.

They are no pack of lies, no lies are among them.
By land-line, *the woman who never sleeps* drapes

her voice beneath the weight of snow and will not
be silenced of her winter's snake-oil contentions.

One could do worse than to turn away
from the window. Falseness, iced in a chill of loss. A self

gone yet further north for insufficiency of reason.
With no moon tonight, sore else will be seen undone.

Owls' Eggs

Tight to a curve by busload in deep winter,
a window-fog of unbearably young, late
in the day, turns sun-streaked, flared as copper-sheet.

Harsh is the word when word is called for to be
sent on ahead, as when the severity
of childhood tends first toward home. There was a girl

earlier, tall and with yellow hair, gliding
down the aisles of fruit, among the peach bins, by bins
of fair-weather grapes and mangoes commuted

of climate, who turned, who came up in profile
of her near-side of face where she was backswept
by a pigment of skin like over-boiling

that scalds and leaves the self in veiled revision.
In a time before words could make a mirror
of her, this was while she was still to be safe

at home. She had glided like the young of owls
fledged out in the raw of winter, when they fly
down through the balsams. When all was her forest.

Canyonland Under Clerical Scrutiny

There is no hidden accommodation in
the hollow of what some say, no cache carved out

to be found unexpectedly, like one cut
into the pages of a nightstand scripture.

Of Vision which has arrived outside of town
now, in broad daylight by motorcade, to stake

big-top tents in field-weeds, there is little to
be said generously, by human nature.

I have not failed, always, when it comes to acts
of toleration. There have been times of shale

and sure-footing I have held to as being
true, those a ganglion sense of childhood twists

itself into. I remember the canyon
of uncloven hooves, of pack-burros packing

out facts accrued on both, slung sides as they had
continued amid mounting evidence, up

and down. It seemed a certainty that they would
not falter, nor was it as though they had not

climbed up to the rim before, some countless times
over, without much in the way of mishap,

as they were ones to keep to realizations,
not to be convinced away from what they knew,

unlike some who learn everything the hard way
by lesson-teaching, free from the empiric,

Canyonland Under Clerical Scrutiny

and besides, you could see them rise up out of
the short grass on long legs as they were born, as

thinking comes, almost in process. You may hear
of rogue coyotes out for ritual kill,

of fit herds driven blind and cliffward – it takes
no burrow-judge of what lies there, in-between

the ears, in the soul-engulfing eyes, to say
it is written elsewhere that clarity once

was there for the finding, in shallow pools where
a water-lens is a rouge-cloth taken to

washed-over stones, and here they come to drink from.
On the green, to speak is to step wirelessly

to the microphone, to sound as coyotes
sound gone hog-wild and low to the ground. As one

not unpracticed in stepping over rattlers
in a nest, I tend toward the stir of dry leaves

in warning, as some have no idea. I have
gone so blindly forth, into the bottomland

between the two schools of sunrise and setting,
toward madder-rose and sorrow's relinquishing

of low horizon; toward citrine's outermost
peel where twilight curls undone. Of a darkness

full of eyes, of its bone worried by, of some
who have no fire to be argued away from.

Mother of Richard

Early on in the woods, we have been speaking
of when, by which hour, by the blood-black grease gun
of predation the honed rake of incisors

on a Tigercat track-saw has been known to
throw an entire tree through a person. Not
without cause does a logger-mother bring her

knitting with her into the woods, as she is
moved by the larval form of likelihood, by
that which her skin feels crawling. In the moonless

now, it is time for her son Richard to put
Venus over his spear-shoulder, in the hour
of stumpage, to speak away timber gone rogue

as it falls, the suction of blue marine clay
known to take a machine down whole, the person
in it. I have found it best to believe in

next to nothing, only the moving warm front
of narration as he knows it to muscle
its way up against masses of chill, speaking

with his helmet in his hands of those who come
with still larger excavation equipment,
praise for those who stay until the sun goes down,

while the mother of him comes to have the facts
brought to her out of the undergrowth feet first,
to wait in the truck cab as she would beside

her fire in an earlier story, while I,
blood-mother of not anyone, will be off-
boiling fruit and stain, pressed through the sieve of it.

Just Above the Water

All is factorial off beyond five times,
and redundant in memorization. So
I'm told, she was told once or more so, fifteen
is out as age-related in noun-form by
parenthood, and now is no more a subject

now. There was a time when I would have asked if,
at daybreak, when nightjars take to the brush, would
now become scaled down to her, fit to the length
of her forearms along the windowsill. Who
could be so young for mothering was given

then as good as gone. Now, who can say by noon
she will not be spooling a fly-rod off through
the pitch-pines to cast her own long following
just above the water. For all the arm she
puts it through does the known world know her more so.

William in Undermeal Atmosphere

When he was one of us, once more in September
when the livestock fair was done with, when
jewel-jars and sour-brined had gone down
to cellar shelves and the pulp shavings

had been swept over, when we were all again
in close-fitting shoes, sent out with agate-sacks
for school with a porch-mat, above us
on the wild hill, the grass would be in seed-heads

and hip-high, past the time of night-pasture,
when the cattle there would be dry and few.
From where you could see a life outlined,
as his was, given perspective apart from

the apple-scented idyll of childhood.
From where he didn't say, but he saw
as from a hill the way the steepled village
lay claim to him, upstream from the jack-

raftered bridge along the back street
where the river was, the kitchen light-switch
lifting out of its surround of pattern
in the papered wall, a faltering of stain

to thicker lipids. In a motherless, in the dust
of one who had died not recently, daylight left off
there like the rind of his own cooking, past
salt-curings, a ruining of coffee, of jarred meats

given benefit of condiments, past the saddened
father-specter elbowed down among a tapering
of bottles' clotted rings, in weakened northlight
through the screen door. Where pity was long since

William in Undermeal Atmosphere

pulled out from under with the oilcloth, to make
a place for. Here, and then far elsewhere, endlessly
at arm's-length from us. From the first, keeping us
from the harm that did or did not happen there.

Soft-Footed Fictions

In which the moon comes up through the trees breathless,
as if it had never felt the rise before.
It's in some other time that I let it break
treeline ahead of when I go unrolling
my whole emballage of tools. Which is to say,

to rework the sheen of the moon's perfection
as by a directive, to say it could yet
be improved upon is as with so many
memories, those with a surround that later
on looks dim and unconvincing, those that need

taking down to the sard, to raise the relief
they sit in. The perfect ice is done. This was
back in a time before wintering owls had
started to sing on the Nesting Place of Crows
River, when ice flash-formed to a calm so deep

it spooled away the cutting edge of friction
as with the state someone's death brings you into
before you hear the knock at your door, before
you know it more than in your marrow. Of ice
as smooth as it would get only once as far

as I can remember. There I was, which is
to say, with the moonlight *glancing* off my blades
like the limited entitlement to what
can be seen in the beforehand. Like the miles
of fiction about to be stripped by houselights,

by hovering destination raising its
backdraft of wings, memory, the upstream stride
of it, had soft-footed out ahead. To know
of no village square to arrive at, know time
would be turning back on a dime before that.

Of Schoolroom Ceremony

It was in a softened silence he appeared,
cautious as a shadow-line across the jamb

and uncertain as parts of speech, the parent
of a back-row boy. And there he waited long

in the doorway as one unused to having
eyes upon him, where he had gathered courage

about him, coarse-cut in a local millrace
wool family suit. All by invitation,

and by its parenthetical rescinding,
he lingered as one for whom realization

comes after, in a doorway, with a sheetcake
held forth. If I were not so drawn to the gray

of eyes that recall kindness distantly, to
kinship's pain, I forget where that would get me.

Mourning Dove by Herself

She would be no more than sorely alone
were it not for singing into the fog

as it sits close around her like her kind
who dampen the off-note

before it starts speaking for her
on its own again. It is for the fog,

now, to mute the sound
like the pink of a hound-horn, half gone

in the hills to say where the fox went.
Last summer has flattened an impression

beneath both her wings: her twin, pin-feathered young
were squirrel-tossed from a height

of pine to fall its trunk-length
with no flight-span. Nothing since

has made them less pocketed to her
than pitch with all its time-fixing.

Everything she sings slow-swings
like a gate closing. In the fog,

each long-following phrase
is one more thing she cannot cross off her list.

She is not finished. She will have no one
to sing to once she is through with this.

Children in Hurricane Weather

Long after, when they return to you, what choice
do they then have but to come to you faceless
through an open door, not unlike leaves blown in.

We have not been given any heaven here,
nor can I say it is not they, in autumn,
who move across the floor so that the windrows

of pine seeds shift all to the far side, breathless.
By now, you've long caught me here by your bass line
dropped after them through the choke-weeds down-streaming.

When you become lost to them, yourself faceless
in autumn, the brood-chicks in the shagbark woods
will once more be full grown. By then, the water

will be perched upland, lingering in high-pitched
tenor of loss. By when the stick-work dams burst
in erosion of cut-banks, in undoing

the soul-rim of you by largo of floodtime,
there may be no other way of brothering
left you. It's a thin grey line that has been drawn

like a string pulling, as on a toy boat dropped
from a bridge railing, so that by evening,
drag chains come echoing back over childhood,

only, when have you not known sound to finger
impingements on the air, bring salts through cell walls?
The last one in rides a string down right through it.

Autumn's Modular Elliptic Curves

Oaks, in the end, some beech and aspen
come to understate and then crowd out
the sharper tones of sugar maple and box elder.
There is a plan afoot, and brilliance decides
to lie more thickly in the leaf. Nothing

quells the ever-sorrowed of late fall,
irremediable as the speech disorder
some must live with, slower, as with
ochre, slower than russet rising out
of a mist. Little more was there than

a slur of distinction, and now the season
is no longer the field-cricket's autumn, literary
and photogenic. When late fall arrives late, it is
as fluid as twilight and as though it had never been
elsewhere. All of sentiment holds the soul

here, and meanwhile its proof is heaped
and reamed in mathematical formulae.
They scroll collectively to give it shape,
as eddied leaves will shape a stream before it
cascades in a change of state. And where you can

see the hillsides through the foliage,
where the crowns take on the curve
of deer-flank in descent, belonging
is drawn to scale, measured like mist
and speechless, unpronounceable as the *I*.

Hayfields, Height-of-Land

To continue, to go beyond the slowdown
of wheel, beyond its halt of twisted spokes, to
keep on from its faltered spin of collision

now that you're gone, were gone in an instant, in
the collective we rise to the crest of hill
known to your plain-spoken childhood. We come to

return you to the subjunctive, here above
the clear possibilities of home-hayfields
as mid-summer frontage to the spectacle

of small hills at large and perpetually
untroubling. That we last spoke of the raw edge
of an oil spill, abrupt and definitive

as the umber border of a southern state
colored in, gone abroad as a wall-map's myth
of country in a child's high-gabled room, that

was just the beginning. Hope, was said, as when
you could fly beyond that edge, further out where
the blue swells outride all wreckage, where again

the chunky gannets wheel and land. I could not
wish for you that you had been held by the heel
and plunged like Achilles into an August

bronzed cancellation of harm, without which hope
sits sprung of risk's horizon to set out from.
Horizon, rim of a thumb-rule where harm is

as good as gone. What damaging has not now
spent itself as would one more small appliance
at its far wall-socket end, run out of reach

Hayfields, Height-of-Land

of you on the meter spinning? Where you are
you are wholly here in these height-of-land fields,
your whistle-grass sound, our present tense of you.

Notes

The idea being presented in "The Far Beyond with Indigo Buntings" is based on research conducted with this species by ornithologist Stephen Emlen, who defined what he called their use of a *star compass*. His experiments revealed a process that requires "learning how to learn," as opposed to genetically inheriting knowledge, which in the Buntings' case involves the ability to recognize and set a course by constellations.

"Winter School" and "Of Winter School, of Irene" were suggested in part by words attributed to Joseph Webster (1772–1810) as said in summary of his half-brother, "Dan was sent to school that he might get as much knowledge as the other boys." The quotation appears in Dearborn, Adams, and Rolfe's, *The History of Salisbury New Hampshire* (William E. Moore, printer, Manchester, N.H., 1890.)

"The Small Sparrows of the Spandrels" draws from ideas brought together by Thomas Nagel in *Mind and Cosmos: Why the Materialistic Neo-Darwinian Conception of Nature is Almost Certainly False* and his reference to an analogy involving the spandrels of San Marcos as developed by Stephen Jay Gould and Richard C. Lewontin.

In "Where Antlers Are Left," the shepherd-legends mentioned are those of the shepherd-god Dumuzi texts, Sumerian poetry thought to have been written toward the end of the third millennium B.C.

The title and spirit of "To Be Shaken out of a Life" is based on the phrase quoted from Andrew Shanks' *God & Modernity*.

The title "Autumn's Modular Elliptic Curves" references Fermat's Last Theorem (Pierre de Fermat, 1601–1665).

A Note About the Author

Audrey Bohanan was born in 1948 in central-southern New Hampshire, where she also spent her childhood, growing up on one of the state's few remaining family farms. Educated at the University of New Hampshire and a graduate of the Vermont College MFA in Writing Program, she has taught writing and poetry for The Johns Hopkins University and Champlain College for many years, and also teaches privately and runs workshops in her local area. In addition to her career in poetry, she earlier served an apprenticeship in the printing industry and journeyed in a shop transitioning from hot-metal typography to digital print. She is married to the furniture-maker and musician Jeff Lind. Having moved to coastal Maine in the mid-1970s, they live and work off-the-grid on a piece of backland devoted to tree growth and wildlife habitat.

Other Books from Waywiser

POETRY
Austin Allen, *Pleasures of the Game*
Al Alvarez, *New & Selected Poems*
Chris Andrews, *Lime Green Chair*
George Bradley, *A Few of Her Secrets*
Geoffrey Brock, *Voices Bright Flags*
Christopher Cessac, *The Youngest Ocean*
Robert Conquest, *Blokelore & Blokesongs*
Robert Conquest, *Penultimata*
Morri Creech, *Blue Rooms*
Morri Creech, *Field Knowledge*
Morri Creech, *The Sleep of Reason*
Peter Dale, *One Another*
Erica Dawson, *Big-Eyed Afraid*
B. H. Fairchild, *The Art of the Lathe*
David Ferry, *On This Side of the River: Selected Poems*
Daniel Groves & Greg Williamson, eds., *Jiggery-Pokery Semicentennial*
Jeffrey Harrison, *The Names of Things: New & Selected Poems*
Joseph Harrison, *Identity Theft*
Joseph Harrison, *Shakespeare's Horse*
Joseph Harrison, *Someone Else's Name*
Joseph Harrison, ed., *The Hecht Prize Anthology, 2005-2009*
Anthony Hecht, *Collected Later Poems*
Anthony Hecht, *The Darkness and the Light*
Jaimee Hills, *How to Avoid Speaking*
Hilary S. Jacqmin, *Missing Persons*
Carrie Jerrell, *After the Revival*
Stephen Kampa, *Articulate as Rain*
Stephen Kampa, *Bachelor Pad*
Rose Kelleher, *Bundle o' Tinder*
Mark Kraushaar, *The Uncertainty Principle*
Matthew Ladd, *The Book of Emblems*
J. D. McClatchy, *Plundered Hearts: New and Selected Poems*
Dora Malech, *Shore Ordered Ocean*
Jérôme Luc Martin, *The Gardening Fires: Sonnets and Fragments*
Eric McHenry, *Odd Evening*
Eric McHenry, *Potscrubber Lullabies*
Eric McHenry and Nicholas Garland, *Mommy Daddy Evan Sage*
Timothy Murphy, *Very Far North*
Ian Parks, *Shell Island*
V. Penelope Pelizzon, *Whose Flesh is Flame, Whose Bone is Time*
Chris Preddle, *Cattle Console Him*
Shelley Puhak, *Guinevere in Baltimore*
Christopher Ricks, ed., *Joining Music with Reason:*

Other Books from Waywiser

34 Poets, British and American, Oxford 2004-2009
Daniel Rifenburgh, *Advent*
Mary Jo Salter, *It's Hard to Say: Selected Poems*
W. D. Snodgrass, *Not for Specialists: New & Selected Poems*
Mark Strand, *Almost Invisible*
Mark Strand, *Blizzard of One*
Bradford Gray Telford, *Perfect Hurt*
Matthew Thorburn, *This Time Tomorrow*
Cody Walker, *Shuffle and Breakdown*
Cody Walker, *The Self-Styled No-Child*
Cody Walker, *The Trumpiad*
Deborah Warren, *The Size of Happiness*
Clive Watkins, *Already the Flames*
Clive Watkins, *Jigsaw*
Richard Wilbur, *Anterooms*
Richard Wilbur, *Mayflies*
Richard Wilbur, *Collected Poems 1943-2004*
Norman Williams, *One Unblinking Eye*
Greg Williamson, *A Most Marvelous Piece of Luck*
Greg Williamson, *The Hole Story of Kirby the Sneak and Arlo the True*
Stephen Yenser, *Stone Fruit*

FICTION

Gregory Heath, *The Entire Animal*
Mary Elizabeth Pope, *Divining Venus*
K. M. Ross, *The Blinding Walk*
Gabriel Roth, *The Unknowns**
Matthew Yorke, *Chancing It*

ILLUSTRATED

Nicholas Garland, *I wish ...*
Eric McHenry and Nicholas Garland, *Mommy Daddy Evan Sage*
Greg Williamson, *The Hole Story of Kirby the Sneak and Arlo the True*

NON-FICTION

Neil Berry, *Articles of Faith: The Story of British Intellectual Journalism*
Mark Ford, *A Driftwood Altar: Essays and Reviews*
Philip Hoy, ed., *A Bountiful Harvest:*
The Correspondence of Anthony Hecht and William L. MacDonald
Richard Wollheim, *Germs: A Memoir of Childhood*

* Co-published with Picador